Table of Contents

Traders and investors do a phenomenal job of acquiring information to improve their technical acumen. We practice our knowledge until we become masters of this information, but what we often forget is to master ourselves—by this I mean our thoughts and impulses. This lack of self mastery is what causes for some traders to experience the pain of failure when implementing their strategies during the move from paper trading to live executions.

The complex internal dialogue that happens inside our head is often what differentiates an amateur trader from a professional. A master trader is calm when the pressure is turned on, and able to use their knowledge effectively to turn profits on a consistent basis. In this book we are going to explore common phrases like "leave your emotions at the door", and that if you want to be successful at trading you need to "control your emotions".

I am sure that you have both heard and read time and time again that in order to be successful at trading you need to be an unemotional person, but is this actually good advice? Not if you consider logic, rational, and sound judgment to be emotions. Let's explore this concept in greater detail. Trading is a highly stressful occupation that requires intense focus and a high level of determination to succeed. You need to be rational about your capital, the wins and losses of money, and you need to come to terms with the very likely possibility of losing everything.

Type A Personalities and Trading

Traders are very intelligent people, who often have a background in business. They are frequently individuals who were successful entrepreneurs in other realms of business. They usually have a Type A personality and a winning "can do" attitude. What exactly is a person that exhibits a Type A personality you ask?—this is an individual that portrays alpha characteristics such as:

- Extremely ambitious in all realms of life
- Rigidly organized and methodical
- Frequently high achieving workaholics
- To the point, and very concerned about time management
- Won't take no for an answer
- "I want it done yesterday"

An individual with a Type A personality does well in business because they have extremely strong will power, and uses their immense mental strength and resolve to make things happen.

Type A people are very successful in business, but unfortunately this success does not translate well into trading and is their Achilles' heel, because they always feel a sense of urgency to be active all the time, and their internal dialogue is often "I need to be trading to be trading".

The Type A's mental disposition sets up the foundation for extremely aggressive trading strategies that cause these people to start chasing trades, and these people very quickly become victims of impulsive trades, and revenge trading—ultimately causing them to overtrade. This sense of urgency to act and "do something, anything" leads individuals to start seeing setups where there are no real profitable setups. They hastily get into a trade that they think is a fantastic idea at the time, shortly after they are knocked out, and then they wonder what happened? They start to think what in their mind caused them to jump into that fatal trade? They convince themselves that they will be more patient "next time", and they try even harder and harder to control their emotions which eventually always ends up hijacking their thinking and soon they find themselves blowing the next trade, *again*.

So why is it that the Type A keeps failing again and again, why is it that these people who are so successful with their immense mental strength and will power unable to control the outcome of their trades? Well that is just it, isn't it? These people are so focused on controlling their emotions and the outcome of their trades that they forget to control the one thing that they actually can control in trading, the *process* of how they execute the trade.

Trader's often fall into the trap of trying to control their emotions, without appreciating the fact that emotions are truly biological in nature. You see, emotions are hard wired into our DNA, we are the embodiment of our emotions, and it is what makes us human. Have you ever taken note of what you feel when you enter a trade? That stress in your chest, the increased heart rate, and possible rocking leg and tapping foot? These are all things that we can observe and take note of as our emotions start to slowly take over our thinking and start to affect our performance in trading.

We have to come to grips with the fact that making a mistake while trading can cost us money, a lot of money—and this is what subconsciously triggers the emotional response. The acute difference between an amateur and a professional trader is that the professional does not feel shame or want to get revenge if they succumb to a string of losses, and conversely does not feel high as a kite and overly confident if they have serial gains. The professional understands that being excited by a number of consecutive back to back gains is actually fatal; it is the sign that the emotions have hijacked the mind.

Understanding the Emotional Hijacking

We are logical beings, so how exactly does a hijacking by emotion occur?

Take a look at the image above. We like to believe that if we encounter an obstacle like a fire, we will act in a logical manner and use the sensory data available to us to properly assess the circumstances, and make a rational decision to deal with the situation with our available resources in a way that will provide us with the most beneficial outcome.

But in reality if there was a fire, we don't stop to think, without even thinking when we see the danger our limbic system (emotional brain) becomes activated and we go into an automated "fear response" to either fight or take flight from the danger. In the case of the fire, we run from it.

The problem is that this almost reflex like mechanism for an actual biological threat is nearly identical to what happens to us during psychological discomfort from trading. Each time that you are hit with a trading loss, or there is the potential risk of experiencing something that can negatively affect your portfolio's capital, our limbic system kicks in— and this is because this system cannot discriminate between a biological threat like a fire, and what is just psychological discomfort. Your ability to think rationally, assess the situation, and work in a decisive manner becomes compromised the instant you face the unknown and are unable to control your outcome. Your mind becomes short circuited and you act with a fearful emotion that clouds your judgment and you begin to make the same mistakes again.

So how do we begin to overcome this challenge that plagues us again and again? The first step is to accept that all emotions are <u>not</u> psychological, rather they are biological in nature and that is why it is *impossible* to trade without emotion—trying to suppress your emotions will only lead to financial ruin. You are under a constant state of stress and pressure to perform rationally, it's just a fact...accept it. The integral fact that differentiates the winning trader from the losing one who blows up their account is that the winner understands emotions and focuses on controlling the process, rather than the outcome. When you put all of your energy on the process and your methods, you will start to gain an edge on the markets.

The Anatomy of an Emotion

Let's dive deeper by deconstructing an emotion, what exactly is an emotion? The language of the brain is electrical activity, this is fact. An emotion is simply an affective state of consciousness that is encoded into that electrical activity. What you have to understand as a trader is that you have the "brain", and you have the "mind". The brain's language is electrical activity through impulses, and the mind's language is thought. The transformation of the massive amounts of electrical activity shapes our *thinking* mind, and whenever you have an acute interruption of that balance and homeostasis you get an emotion. In other words, if you have any slight deviation in the already established standard patterns of your environment, you will feel an emotion.

Let us imagine for a moment that it is Monday morning and you boot up your computer just before the markets open. You are calm and collected as you start to review your chart patterns from last week for your favourite stock. The instant that the opening bell rings and your indicators start to fire off, and you start to see all the bright colours and numbers flashing on your screen, that homeostasis becomes disrupted. Suddenly you are exposed to risk and there is action. Should I take a position, or should I wait? You will start to experience emotions because of that unknown factor that you now have to manage.

Let's take a closer look at the mechanism by which emotions are generated or created.

Stage 1

The first stage is for you to reach a certain threshold of arousal. What I mean by this is that some external event has to stimulate you, for example: a sudden dip or rise in a stock price. There are some symptoms associated with this stage such as,

- Tensioning in your body, usually the chest or shoulders
- Noticeable rise in heartbeat
- Fixation of eyes, or tunnel vision
- Irritability

As I mentioned before, emotions are biological, and not psychological—once an emotion has been expressed it is not possible to interrupt it. However, we can interrupt the buildup of an emotion at Stage 1, more on this later.

Stage 2

After we have exceeded the threshold level the emotion will fire, just like a nerve impulse. Think of it as a dam that can no longer hold in the water and then bursts, or a light switch that is flicked from the "off" position to the "on" position.

At this stage you will feel the emotion rushing through your body, flooding your entire system and altering how you see and perceive the world. Most traders try to suppress their feelings and emotions when they are at this stage, but it is too late. The electrical activity in your brain is already charged to make you act in a certain way, and it gives you the motivation to act in accordance with the classic "fight or flight" approach to handle a dangerous situation,

- *Fight*: You find yourself putting in losing trade after losing trade just trying to "make back" what you lost to the market.
- *Flight*: Locking down a position early because you are afraid that you might lose money, or conversely because you are afraid you might lose your profits (only to watch the stock shoot up after you sell).

In the flight scenario you are avoiding the dangerous situation by being hesitant to see what happens if you wait, and instead opt to lock down your trade, and conversely in the fight scenario you become aggressive and start to over trade and revenge trade just to get even. The interesting thing with trading is that it exposes our flaws. If you haven't developed your emotional intelligence to appropriately deal with pressure, you will come undone as soon as you are exposed to the unknown and uncertainty of a position on the market.

The major problem here is that this leads many traders to feel inadequate, powerless and unworthy of success. They feel like they can never be consistently profitable. A trader who allows himself to get to Stage 2 is like the person that sees the fire, and the left brain instantly makes a decision for the right brain to get them out of the danger zone—and sometimes that decision no matter how irrational, makes sense at that moment in time (this explains why people often jump out of burning high rise buildings, only to die upon impact). Sometimes these "rational" decisions happen again and again, and that is what causes your account balance to dwindle.

The euphoria of being in the trade is what leads to overtrading, let's face it, it is not fun just sitting around and staring at charts just waiting around for something to happen. When we are in a state of euphoria we have a lot of dopamine and testosterone surging through our system, and when we are afraid we will have cortisol—and these hormones are what help to push on the emotions.

A person who has high emotional intelligence realizes that by understanding what they are thinking, and why, lets them to positively impact their outcome—and this is what makes a great trader. The difference between the person making lots of money from those who are broke is that the one who is making a lot of money is not necessarily smarter or more knowledgeable about trading, they are just better at managing their emotions and not always trying to suppress this biological certainty.

So now that we have acknowledged that developing our emotional intelligence commences when we first acknowledge that we are emotional organisms, we have to work on managing these emotions. Not just during losses, but during wins too. Nothing says the kiss of death like feeling high and mighty because of a winning streak. You start to think about that new sports car that you are going to buy, or that dream vacation that you are going to take. This overconfidence can lead to overtrading to get to your goal faster, which will inevitably lead to miscalculations of risk, and we know what happens then.

Dealing with Chaos and Uncertainty

Trading is all about dealing with uncertainty and managing chaotic situations. These situations breed confusion. Let me explain with the aid of the diagram below.

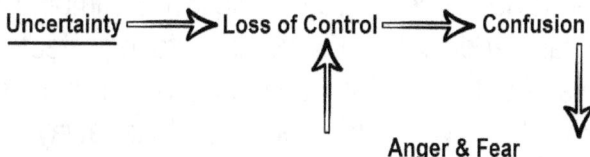

When faced with uncertainty we tend to feel like we have lost control, and this leads to confusion. This confusion is essentially the result of not having control of the trade—this then short circuits our thinking and we react to the psychological discomfort as if it were a biological threat...and then the anger and fear sets in, further clouding our judgment and leading us to lose more control of the situation. While this is happening, more uncertainty is being fed into the system by way of more movement on the stock charts.

So let us more closely examine the different types of negative trading personas that we can take on when trading.

Overtrading

This is one of the deadliest sins and results from the excitement of chasing the trade for action. A lot of traders have a sense of urgency to act, and while this behaviour can be rewarding while climbing the corporate ladder, it can have devastating effects for traders. Fueled on by dopamine, overtrading can quickly cloud your judgment and take away your impartiality when viewing charts.

Overtraders lack the discipline to be patient and wait for setups with high probabilities. Patience will always win more money than full on aggression. When you allow yourself to feel good and overconfident about a trade, the euphoria that starts to set in and will kill your winning streak and destroy your overall performance.

Impulsive Trading

This builds upon overtrading, as a large percentage of impulsive trades result from overconfidence. This happens when you see something on the charts and start thinking that you are going to win, and so your pulse accelerates, you feel euphoria as the dopamine kicks in and so you enter a trade without thinking it through properly. You then quickly realize that you miscalculated your risk as the stock moves the other way, and you quickly go from being an overconfident trader to someone who is just praying and begging to get their money back.

Revenge Trading

This sort of trading happens when you are already down on your position(s). If you reflect back to the diagram at the beginning of this section you will see the label "Anger & Fear", and it is this anger from feeling powerless that spurs you on to get back into the game and try to win everything back. The threat of catastrophic ruin causes you to fight back, and hard, instead of taking flight. The rage in your system causes you to take irrational positions that inevitably results in more loss of control—it truly is a vicious cycle.

There is Hope!

The good news is that there is hope! You can in fact work on reprogramming your mind. Fear and other emotions are actually very useful when used in moderation and when we can modulate the intensity without letting it overwhelm and take over and cloud our judgment. Fear can be used to help us be more cautious and calculate and recalculate our positions. Euphoria on the other hand is an emotion that is very dangerous for traders because it makes you feel like you are in the zone, but really you are so far from it. Euphoria is what turns the mathematical process of trading, throws out all the logic, and turns it into pure gambling.

Accept that you are not seeing the markets as they are, but rather through the coloured lenses of your emotions. Your brain is taking in data from the charts, and you are interpreting this data and interacting with this information to make your own inputs into the market. Remember the following point, it is so important that I will underline it for you, <u>You don't first see and then believe, you first believe and then you see</u>. Think about that for a moment, and reflect on what I just wrote. When you start to become consciously aware of this fact you will see that the effectiveness of your trading will reflect positively on the value of your trading account.

You can lie to yourself about your trading, and you can lie to others about your trading, but your trading account will always tell the truth about your real performance. So what can you do to improve your trading?

Take a look at your posture right now. Are you sitting up straight, or are you slouched? If you are slouched, practice sitting up straight because this allows more air to flow into the lower extremities of your lung—and this will give more oxygen to the brain. Trading is a thinking exercise. Always be conscious of your posture when sitting at your trading desk, this will go a long way towards your improvement.

Now think for a moment what do you do when you have a losing trade. Think about it. What *should* you do when you lose? What do we do to kids when they misbehave?—we give them a time out. If you have a losing trade you will have a lot of hormones surging through your body and you need to step away from your computer so that you can cool down mentally. You need to extinguish the trigger for the emotions that you are experiencing. It takes a good 25-40minutes to flush that negative chemistry out of your system. I like to wash my cars or do some quick exercises, say 40 situps followed by 40 pushups and a brisk stroll around the city block. This will do wonders to flush out that negative chemistry, and then you will be ready to take a deep breath and sit back down more focused, and you are off to the races again!

From time to time you will also need to do some introspection and see how you are doing on the "inside". If you feel the tension setting in, you can benefit from some emotion regulation and relaxation therapy.

Relaxation Therapy	
Step 1	Close your eyes and breathe in. Feel your chest start to expand.
Step 2	Hold this position for five seconds.
Step 3	Slowly release the air from your chest cavity and be consciously aware of this. Imagine that you are like a big balloon that is slowly deflating.
Step 4	As you slowly release air feel your muscles lose their tension. Drain all the tension away from your body, feel it evaporate until your body becomes lose and relaxed.

This activity is easy to do and shouldn't take more than ten minutes, repeat as necessary. After completing this exercise you will find that you are calmer, and you will have less self limiting beliefs. You will be more relaxed and attentive.

Stop deceiving yourself, be honest and submit yourself fully to learning the process of trading rather than trying to suppress your human emotions. Be mindful of the fact that only you sabotage your own trading. Don't subscribe to the false idea that you have to be "trading to be trading", rather you have to be patient and wait like the viper that only strikes when certain that it can catch its prey. Don't despair; soon you too will be a profitable trader.